AF483512

JEREMIAH

A Character Study

Register This New Book

Benefits of Registering*

- ✓ FREE **replacements** of lost or damaged books

- ✓ FREE **audiobook** – *Pilgrim's Progress,* audiobook edition

- ✓ FREE information about new titles and other **freebies**

www.anekopress.com/new-book-registration

*See our website for requirements and limitations.

JEREMIAH

— A Character Study —

WILLIAM G.
BALLANTINE

Jeremiah

© 2026 by Aneko Press

All rights reserved. First edition 1892.

Revisions copyright 2026.

Cover Designer: J. Martin

Editor: P. Miller

Aneko Press

www.anekopress.com

inquiries@anekopress.com

Aneko Press, Life Sentence Publishing, and our logos are trademarks of

Life Sentence Publishing, Inc.
203 E. Birch Street
P.O. Box 652
Abbotsford, WI 54405

RELIGION / Christian Living / Spiritual Growth

Paperback ISBN: 979-8-88936-573-0

eBook ISBN: 979-8-88936-574-7

10   9   8   7   6   5   4   3   2   1

Available where books are sold

JEREMIAH

Jeremiah is the most misunderstood of all the great men in history. To be one of the healthiest of men and to be thought morbid, to be one of the strongest and to be thought weak, to be one of the bravest and to be thought fainthearted, to be a giant and to be thought small, has been his hard fortune.

We Americans, with our national temperament and popular philosophy, find it nearly impossible to understand Jeremiah. To truly understand him implies such a profound insight into human character, into the lessons of the past and the facts of the present, into the religious history of the race and the perils of today, as our happy circumstances and prosperous material civilization with difficulty allow. To understand Jeremiah is to understand the world's need of Christ.

Jeremiah is the weeping prophet, the commonly

accepted author of the book of Lamentations. Of all the prophetic biblical writings, his book is the longest and the gloomiest. We facetiously call any downcast utterance, such as a homesick letter or a pessimistic editorial, a "Jeremiad." Jeremiah is the man who said, *Oh that my head were waters, and mine eyes a fountain of tears, that I might weep day and night for the slain of the daughter of my people! Oh that I had in the wilderness a lodging place of wayfaring men; that I might leave my people and go from them!* (Jeremiah 9:1-2).

Popularly, Jeremiah is looked upon as a man naturally depressed – a man whose liver was probably out of order, a man to whom one might have recommended horseback exercise, a little more general society, a little more recreation, and perhaps a book from some popular humorist after dinner. He is certainly thought to be one of those men whose characters serve rather as a warning of "how not to do it" than as examples for imitation. So much is said nowadays about making religion attractive and carrying sunshine in the face that we condemn Jeremiah at sight, unheard. We contrast him disparagingly with Moses, Joshua, Samuel, Elijah, and Paul. They were founders, builders, inspirers, leaders, and conquerors. Jeremiah was only a weeping hypochondriac, foretelling calamity and wringing his hands when it came.

But this judgment is in the highest degree false and unjust, a cruel wrong to Jeremiah, and a discredit to our own understanding. When we think of Jeremiah, let us think of him as we do of the Titan Prometheus in the tragedy of Aeschylus, chained upon the rock of Caucasus with the insatiable vulture tearing his vitals, unconquerable, but crying in his anguish:

> Woe, woe, today's woe and the coming morrow's
> I cover with one groan!
> And where is found for me
> A limit to these sorrows?
> Under earth, under Hades,
> Where the home of the shade is,
> All into the deep, deep Tartarus,
> I would he had hurled me down!
> I would he had plunged me fastened thus
> In the knotted chain with the savage clang
> All into the dark, where there should be none,
> Neither God nor another, to laugh and to see!
> But now the winds sing through and shake
> The hurtling chains wherein I hang –
> And I, in my naked sorrow, make
> Much mirth for my enemy.[1]

---

1   Mrs. Elizabeth Barrett Browning's translation.

My hope is that a more careful and thoughtful study will make it forever impossible for us to speak jestingly of the tears of Jeremiah.

This prophet had a strange mission to accomplish. It was to interpret and to immortalize in literature the failure of the experiment of a visible, genuine, holy empire. It was Jeremiah's role to feel all the magnificence and glory of the legislation of Moses, of the conquests of Joshua, of the attributes of Samuel, of the royalty of David, Solomon, and Josiah, and then to see all this overwhelmed in darkness because the Jewish people were dishonorably false to themselves and to their God. It was Jeremiah's lot to stand and see the solitary lighthouse, which for centuries had glowed on Mount Zion in the vast sea of ancient heathenism, overthrown and its light quenched.

What was Jeremiah's lifework? It was to pass through and to understand and to feel the saddest and most shameful of all earthly tragedies before that of Calvary – namely, the fall of the Jewish kingdom and the destruction of Solomon's temple. It was his job to preserve for us these dreadful experiences in all their details of guilt and shame.

The human race knows itself and its environment, and its experiences, only in literature. As the sweetness of flowers must be gathered by the bees into their combs before we can possess it as honey, so the lessons of life are ours only as authors have gathered them into books. We see nature through the eyes of the poets, and if it were not for the historians, we would have, as a race, no memory. Men without letters must remain, like the American Indians, on the level of the beavers and the wolves, or sink even below that. Greece began to know herself in Homer's *Iliad and Odyssey.* If, then, the profound significance of the fall of Judah was to be known and felt by its own age, or by succeeding ages, some great soul must taste the bitterness of its dregs, and must immortalize its unparalleled sorrows in a book.

The crudest way to treat a man trembling in anguish under the weight of some real and immeasurable public calamity is to casually assume, without examination, that the trouble is merely in his own imagination. When, with tearful eyes and faltering voice, a message of dreadful significance is delivered, could anything be worse than to turn cheerfully away with the remark that as for ourselves, we believe in a religion of sunshine?

Jeremiah's tragic distinction has been just this – to see the darkest truths and to feel what that truth compelled, and then to be told, "It's just Jeremiah's way. That's just how he is." Thus a careless world tries to lessen the sting of serious reproof. They accuse those who talk of national sins as being naturally judgmental; those who defend truth are interfering; those who speak of divine wrath are themselves naturally vindictive.

As far as we have facts for a judgment, Jeremiah was the healthiest, strongest, bravest, grandest man of Old Testament history. There is not a scrap of evidence that he was anything other than naturally courageous, hopeful, inspired, with a soul as full of song as a bird's, and as receptive and radiant of light as a diamond. Every constraint that we make in estimating his temperament is an unjustified subtraction from the tragic objective truth of history. It is only when we admit what the fall of Judah meant to one so clear-eyed, so wholesome, so adaptable as Jeremiah that we begin to see how dreadful that fall really was.

We may compare Jeremiah in detail with the greatest men in Hebrew history, and always to his advantage. We may take the darkest hour in the life of Moses, of Joshua, of Samuel, of Elijah, or of Paul, and we will find that Jeremiah had a similar experience, only ten times darker. And after such a comparison, we will feel that they all seem weak compared with him.

Take Moses: He was disheartened after the Israelites had made the golden calf at Mount Sinai. Under the threats of divine wrath, his spirit fainted. Alone with God on the top of the mountain, he interceded for the disobedient people. He said, *If thou wilt, forgive their sin – and if not, blot me, I pray thee, out of thy book which thou hast written* (Exodus 32:32). We dare not say what Moses would have done if the strain upon his spirit had been intensified or prolonged. But his prayer was heard, and the people were forgiven.

Jeremiah had a different experience. He was told, *Pray not thou for this people, neither lift up cry nor prayer for them, neither make intercession to me: for I will not hear thee* (Jeremiah 7:16). God said, *Though Moses and Samuel stood before me, yet my mind could not be toward this people: cast them out of my sight and let them go forth* (Jeremiah 15:1). If Moses is majestic in the strength and victory of his intercession, much more is Jeremiah majestic, going forth uncomforted to his long and dreadful work among his doomed fellow countrymen for whom he was not even allowed to pray.

Compare Jeremiah with Joshua. The conqueror of Canaan was surely a man of soldierly mold. But after the defeat of Ai, which followed the sin of Achan in taking a part of the accursed spoil of Jericho, Joshua lay prostrate upon his face upon the ground. *O LORD*, he exclaimed, *what shall I say, when Israel turneth their backs before their enemies!* (Joshua 7:8). This was a single defeat of a small detachment, the loss of thirty-six men, a temporary setback in a victorious career, yet Joshua was utterly prostrated. Jeremiah, though, lived all his life in a community of Achans whose every battle was a defeat and whose certain end was national ruin.

Let us compare Jeremiah with Samuel. Samuel mourned for Saul as Jeremiah did for King Josiah; but it was Samuel's privilege to anoint David, a man after God's own heart, and to lay the foundations for a far more splendid kingdom. How small the sorrows of Samuel, and how large his encouragements, compared with those of Jeremiah! The first great sorrow of Jeremiah's life was the death of good King Josiah at Megiddo in an unwise battle against the Egyptians. Josiah was the last worthy successor of King David, a man of royal nature as well as name. He left a family of notoriously weak and wicked sons who were wholly unworthy to succeed him. As flawed as the nation then was, there was still public sensibility enough to feel that the loss was irreparable. The mourning for King Josiah later became the proverbial example of boundless grief.

During the twenty-two years that intervened between the death of Josiah and the final catastrophe, three of his sons and one grandson successively disgraced the throne. Set up and pulled down by foreign conquerors, each was finally carried away to die in captivity, except Jehoiakim, who was murdered and cast forth with the burial of a donkey. Each of these weaklings during his brief abuse of power had time enough to demonstrate his inability, duplicity, vanity, obstinacy, greed, and impiety. As the full, strong current of the Nile River or the Mississippi River, as it nears the ocean, lessens and divides across the mud flats of a delta, so the royal dynasty of David at the end was lost in these contemptible branches. Through all the slow, heartbreaking steps of this political decadence, Jeremiah went down with his nation into its grave.

Compare Jeremiah with Elijah, who is thought to have been the boldest of the prophets. Elijah was the prototype of the undaunted John the Baptist. His rough camel's-hair coat and leather belt were proper emblems for one before whose rebuke the kings of Israel trembled. Yet Elijah fled away before the threats of Queen Jezebel into the desert, and despondently sat down under a juniper tree and prayed for death. But to him it was revealed that circumstances were not as bad as they seemed. There were still seven thousand men whose knees had not bowed to Baal. Jeremiah, on the contrary, had a divine commission to proclaim: *Run ye to and fro through the streets of Jerusalem, and see now, and know, and seek in the broad places thereof, if ye can find a man, if there be any that executeth judgment, that seeketh the truth: and I will pardon it* (Jeremiah 5:1). What Elijah mistakenly supposed to be his own lot was really the lot of Jeremiah. Still, Jeremiah was not permitted to flee away. Firm at his post where Elijah did not have courage to stand, Jeremiah stood to the bitter end.

Compare Jeremiah with Paul. Paul wrote in one of his letters, *I have great heaviness and continual sorrow in my heart. For I could wish that myself were accursed from Christ for my brethren, my kinsmen according to the flesh* (Romans 9:2-3). But this was only a part of Paul's experience. He had the privilege of going far away from unready Jerusalem to do a work of magnificent effectiveness among the Gentiles, where multitudes of converts became his joy and his crown. Jeremiah, though, through his long ministry, had only the great heaviness and continual sorrow in his heart, and nothing else. His duty was to stay year after year in Jerusalem – rejected, threatened, set in the stocks, cast into the miry dungeon, and repeating over and over a fearful message to unwilling ears, with never the joy of a single success.

Thus, neither Moses, nor Joshua, nor Samuel, nor Elijah, nor Paul were ever subjected to a tenth of what Jeremiah endured. As a sufferer, he stands next to our Lord Himself. Why should we attribute his distress to a dismal predisposition to despair? If he ran from the stern task assigned him, Moses and Isaiah had done the same. If he yielded to discouragement in defeat,

Joshua had done the same. If he longed for a lodge in the wilderness, the bold Elijah had sought the same. If he cursed the day of his birth, Job, the great example of patience, had done the same. If he wept over Jerusalem, so did our Lord. That Jeremiah preserved the sweetness of his affections, the loyalty of his piety, and the boldness of his official testimony to the end argues instead that Jeremiah had a preeminently strong, steadfast, fervent, heroic nature.

That eloquent writer Professor Austin Phelps, in his little book *Studies of the Old Testament*, has, under the title of "The Prophet of the Broken Heart," a highly appreciative chapter about Jeremiah, but is not appreciative enough. He says: "The class of godly men and women of whom Jeremiah is the type possess a very profound style of Christian character. It is not perfect, by any means. We all have an ideal of a certain robust and rounded Christian life superior to theirs. On the whole, Paul was a nobler character than Jeremiah." This comparison seems unjust to us. It lacks perceptiveness of insight into history. Professor Phelps cannot believe that the fall of Judah was in itself as sad as it was. He fails to see how much lighter Paul's trials were than Jeremiah's. We might as well say that Jesus, when He rejoiced in the Spirit, was "more robust and rounded" than when He wept over Jerusalem or agonized in Gethsemane.

Jeremiah was a patriot whose duty it was to discourage national hopes and counsel submission to a foreign foe. It was never his privilege to awaken the national spirit, to fire the hearts of the soldiers of Israel, or to call up the mighty enthusiasm that had carried to victory the armies of the Lord of Hosts in the glorious days of Joshua, Gideon, and David. Though a patriot, he seemed to his fellow citizens to be a traitor, without faith in his country or sympathy for her defenders.

As a prophet, Jeremiah did not have the satisfaction of reforming, inspiring, or leading in anything. He found the whole nation coarse, idolatrous, impure, false, dishonest, murderous, willful, and obstinate. Only Sodom and Gomorrah could furnish a parallel. Jeremiah's work was to predict to these people invasion, famine, pestilence, drought, defeat, captivity, despair, the sack of the city, and the destruction of the temple. No other prophet ever had such a task. Jeremiah said, *I beheld the earth, and, lo, it was without form, and void; and the heavens, and they had no light. I beheld the mountains, and, lo, they trembled, and all the hills moved lightly. I beheld, and, lo, there was no man, and all the birds of the heavens were fled. I beheld, and, lo, the fruitful place was a wilderness, and all the cities thereof were broken down at the presence of the* LORD, *and by his fierce anger* (Jeremiah 4:23-26).

These words probably suggested one of the most dramatic of Lord Byron's poems. With such a grim message, Jeremiah stood through his long ministry like an iron pillar, like a brazen wall, in antagonism to the kings, the princes, the priests, the prophets, and the people (Jeremiah 1:18). Yet naturally, he had the gentle, sympathetic heart of a child. There were prophets enough at that day, high in public esteem, whose smooth eloquence found ready applause. Jeremiah stood alone – not that he was naturally contentious or uncompromising, and not for any reason in himself, but because the others were all wrong, and he was under a divine necessity to stand where he did. Martin Luther, before the diet of Worms, was not more heroically loyal to truth. Jeremiah stood like Abdiel, as John Milton has pictured him among the rebellious angels in his *Paradise Lost*:

> Among innumerable false, unmoved,
> Unshaken, unseduced, unterrified,
> His loyalty he kept, his love, his zeal;
> Nor numbers, nor example, with him wrought
> To swerve from truth, or change his constant mind,
> Though single.

Yet Jeremiah did not meet scorn with "retorted scorn," as Milton said of Abdiel; he met it with tears.

Jeremiah was a lonely man. He had no home into which he could run out of the storms of public life, as into a little sunny harbor of peace. This was not, as Professor Phelps thinks, because his heart was disinclined to share its burden with another, but by divine command. The consolation of wife and children was denied him: *Thou shalt not take thee a wife, neither shalt thou have sons and daughters in this place. For thus saith the* LORD *concerning the sons and concerning the daughters that are born in this place . . . : They shall die of grievous deaths; they shall not be lamented, neither shall they be buried; but they shall be as dung upon the face of the earth* (Jeremiah 16:2-4).

As Jeremiah walked along the streets of Jerusalem and looked into the bright faces of the children, he knew that each of those children was destined for a death of horror. Thus, as a man, Jeremiah must close up his heart and repress all its tenderest affections; as a citizen, he must live in the midst of the murderous treachery of his nearest neighbors; as a patriot, he must stand helpless in sight of the slow destruction of his country; as a prophet, he must warn in vain, and with his unavailing pleas and reproofs add to the guilt of the defiant; and this was so that all time might, through him, feel the doom of unrepentant national sin.

Let us contemplate for a little while this grand figure standing there in the solitude of its grief over the ruins of the noblest experiment of ancient times. There he stands, comparing the divine ideal of a visible kingdom of God on earth with the reality; comparing the possibilities and hopes of the past with the facts of the present and the certainties of the future.

In him we see the dignity of unselfish grief. In him we see the manliness of tears. Looking at him, we see that the broadest, truest, strongest, and bravest may, for that very reason, be the saddest.

America now celebrates the person who is funny. He draws crowds as no one else does. Our speeches are becoming funnier on every public occasion. Reforms must be advocated humorously and the audience kept laughing while their moral sense is alerted to the evils of intemperance or political corruption. This is a national weakness, from which we turn with fresh respect to the sublime seriousness of Jeremiah.

Jeremiah's mood was justified by the facts. It was pushed forward to a healthy, clear-eyed nature by the situation, for there was no bright side to those facts to look upon. To have felt otherwise than Jeremiah did would have argued a little or a frivolous mind, unable or unwilling to see and feel the truth.

Looking at Jeremiah and contemplating the lessons of his tears, we begin to suspect that our unreadiness to understand him may come from the influence on our minds of the popular untruths that pervade the literature of the day. In his presence, the emptiness of these misconceptions become more apparent than ever. Here are some of them:

First Fallacy. "One should always look on the bright side." It is sometimes said that the life of religious people is too serious. But how can that be so if the truth is serious? Many things in this world have no bright side. Can we remember some whom we loved as bright boys twenty years ago, but who slipped into drunkenness and immorality, and died in disgrace when they should have been in the prime of their young manhood? Can we ever remember these people without a great sting of grief?

Second Fallacy. "All things are for the best." This is repeated as if it were a text of Scripture, but there is no such idea in the Bible. Many things are not for the best, but are terribly and completely bad. As a nation, we are sending shiploads of rum into Africa, to add the poison of civilization to the depravity of heathenism in the darkest continent. Is it for the best? Think of our national sins – our profanity, for instance! The air of America, from the Atlantic to the Pacific, is filled every day with profanity. Our teams are harnessed, our cattle herded, our lumber felled, our minerals mined, our ships sailed, and our railroads operated all with unceasing blasphemy. Is it for the best?

Third Fallacy. "Truth is mighty and will prevail." Yes, ultimately, somewhere, but not necessarily here and now. Truth did not prevail in Judea, nor in Assyria, nor in Babylon, nor in Egypt, nor in Greece, nor in Rome. Those nations sank under the weight of their sins. Jeremiah would have said, "Undoubtedly in some distant time and place, God will fulfill Himself in many ways. I feel no uneasiness about God. But my generation, my country, my king, the Jerusalem that I love, this sacred temple, these lovely Judean hills, these men and women and children to whom my heart is bound – for them there is nothing in store but ruin; and therefore I must weep." The certain ultimate victory of truth is distant comfort when those you love are in the armies of error, charging the artillery of God.

Fourth Fallacy. "Great crises always produce great

men." Jeremiah did not find it so. The rule, in fact, is the other way. Even a quick glance across the field of history shows that in most great crises in the past, things have gone wrong due to a lack of men great enough to properly guide them. How could tyranny and ignorance and heathenism prevail now over the majority of the earth if in a thousand crises, nations had not failed to find leaders and defenders of truth?

Fifth Fallacy. "Reformations never roll backward." Jeremiah would have said, "The reformations of Hezekiah and Josiah have gone backward, and people are worse than before." Reformations generally have rolled backward, or at least have stopped rolling forward, which, in the stream of time, is practically backward motion. The saddest thing in modern history is the stoppage and backward movement of the great reformation of Luther and Calvin. Let Bohemia, Poland, Spain, and France say whether reformations ever roll backward.

Sixth Fallacy. "If religion is rightly presented, people will always welcome the preacher." "What is the matter with the ministers?" is a freely raised question. Some say to give young men preparing to preach more practical exercises; some say to give them more drill in the English Bible; some say, more sociology; others say, more public speaking. All agree that some important improvement should be made. But possibly the fault is not in the preachers, but in the people. Jeremiah was the most unpopular preacher in Jerusalem – simply because the people did not want the truth. He failed in Jerusalem for the same reason that Jesus failed in Nazareth and in Capernaum. There is no more reason to think that popular preachers are the best preachers than to think that popular music is the best music. Jeremiah was rejected because God was rejected.

Seventh Fallacy. "In politics, we can rely on the rational second thought of the plain, common people." Our political institutions have given us a wholly unwarranted respect for the majority. All Americans are by education demagogues. When we go to England, nothing strikes us as so surprising and so absurd as the public deference and real consideration accorded to titled men of inferior character. Thomas Jefferson called it "heaping importance upon idiots." However, we treat the majority with the same admiration and the same unreasoning confidence. The majority of Jeremiah's contemporaries were wrong, not merely in head, but in heart. The majority of people have always been wrong.

There is a baseless and thoughtless optimism in our

popular speech and literature that is directly contrary to the plainest teachings of history and of the Bible. We do not have the nerve to admit to ourselves the wickedness of men and the dreadful punishments that they bring down upon themselves. Whoever is brave enough to look facts in the face, and unselfish enough to feel, must carry at all times a weight of dread and grief that is beyond expression in words. This would be insupportable, except that the Christian also has hopes and joys that are even more incomparable. We live, indeed, in brighter days than Jeremiah, in the most favored land, and we behold the wide goodness of the gospel, as well as the ruins of sin. It is right for us to have emotions appropriate to both. It seems to be the purpose of our heavenly Father to sway our hearts with emotions as strong as the tides of the ocean, and thus to make them like His own. The mind of the Christian is held in balance by the same forces that balance the stars in their courses.

Unselfish grief over the ruin of individuals, of generations, and of nations refines the soul, dignifies it, gives it steadiness under temptations, gives it earnestness in the work of life, and brings it into sympathy with Him who wept over Jerusalem.

William G. Ballantine – A Brief Biography

William G. Ballantine (1848–1937) was an American Congregational minister, biblical scholar, and educator whose ministry included the classroom, the pulpit, and the written page. He is remembered today especially for his concise interpretive studies of Old Testament prophets – among them *Jeremiah: A Character Study* – and for his work in Bible teaching and translation.

Records associated with Marietta College place Ballantine among the class of 1868, and later list him with the degrees and honors that marked his growing reputation: an earned A.M., a theological degree from Union Theological Seminary (1872), and subsequent honorary recognitions including the D.D. (1885) and an LL.D. from Western Reserve (1891).

Following seminary, Ballantine pursued advanced study abroad at the University of Leipzig (1872–73), a path taken by many American theologians who wanted first-hand exposure to German scholarship and methods. The same biographical record notes that, in these early years, he participated in the American Palestine Exploration enterprise in 1873, an experience that fit the late–19th-century Protestant impulse to illuminate the Bible through geography, archaeology, and travel narratives.

Ballantine's early professional life shows an unusual breadth. Marietta's catalogue traces his movement through a series of academic posts: he served as acting professor of English at Indiana University (1873); taught science at Ripon College (1874–76); returned to Indiana University as assistant professor of Greek (1876–78); and then joined the faculty of Oberlin Theological Seminary, where he taught in areas spanning classical languages and biblical exegesis. These appointments underscore something characteristic of Ballantine: he belonged to a generation of clergy-scholars for whom Bible study was inseparable from rigorous language work in Greek and Hebrew, and for whom teaching and writing were primary ministerial callings.

Ballantine was married and raised a family, though, like many Protestant scholar-clergy of the late nineteenth century, he left few personal details on record concerning his domestic life. Contemporary institutional catalogues and biographical notices consistently identify him as a married man and indicate that he had children, yet they devote little attention to names or family circumstances, focusing instead on his academic, editorial, and administrative work. This relative silence reflects the conventions of the period, in which a minister's household was assumed rather than described, and private family life was rarely preserved in formal professional memorials. Ballantine's career nevertheless suggests a stable family setting that accompanied his long years of teaching, leadership, and biblical instruction, providing the personal context within which his scholarly and pastoral labors were carried out.

By the 1880s, Ballantine had become influential not only in the classroom but also through print. The Marietta record identifies him as associate editor of *Bibliotheca Sacra* (1884–91), a significant platform for evangelical Protestant scholarship in the period. Editorial work of that sort tended to sharpen a scholar's ability to communicate clearly to pastors and educated lay readers – an ability that becomes evident in the style of Ballantine's own studies.

In 1891, Ballantine's career reached a new level when he was elected (and served) as president of Oberlin College. Oberlin's own historical listings identify him as president from 1891 to 1896. A later archival description from Oberlin notes that he resigned after five years, suggesting a presidency of consequence but relatively limited duration, after which he turned again toward teaching and biblical instruction.

Ballantine's writing on the prophets fits squarely into his wider vocation. His best-known title for many readers, *Jeremiah: A Character Study*, circulated in a small, accessible format and was often paired with a companion piece on Ezekiel. Library catalog records preserve it as part of *Jeremiah, Ezekiel, Two Studies* (published by F. H. Revell in the early 1890s), with the Jeremiah section explicitly titled "a character study" and the Ezekiel section presented as "a literary study." Contemporary scholarly periodicals noticed these booklets, indicating that Ballantine's work was visible within the broader conversation about Old Testament interpretation in his day.

After leaving Oberlin, Ballantine accepted an appointment as Professor of Bible at the YMCA training school in Springfield, Massachusetts (often associated historically with Springfield College). An Oberlin archival description states that he took up this role after resigning the presidency and that he remained connected to that work until his retirement in 1921.

Bibliographic listings attribute to Ballantine *The Riverside New Testament* (a translation published in 1923) as well as *Understanding the Bible* (published in 1925) and other instructional works. While Ballantine's translation work is sometimes discussed in relation to copyright history and later reprints, the essential point is that he spent his post-presidency years pouring his learning into resources intended to help ordinary readers engage Scripture thoughtfully.

Ballantine died in 1937, closing a life that had spanned the Civil War generation's aftermath through the upheavals of the early twentieth century. His legacy is best seen not in one monumental tome, but in the pattern of his service: a scholar-teacher deeply committed to rigorous study and faithful instruction, a churchman who believed biblical study should change how one lives and follows Christ, and a leader who moved from college presidency back into hands-on Christian education. Ballantine approached Scripture not merely as text to be analyzed, but as a living word meant to shape the conscience and courage of God's people – especially in hard times, when prophetic faithfulness is most tested.